MACBETH

ISBN   1 85854 272 3
Published by Brimax Books Ltd, Newmarket, England, CB8 7AU, 1997.
Printed in Hong Kong.

MACBETH

ILLUSTRATED BY ERIC KINCAID

LIGHTNING CRACKLED AND FORKED ACROSS A BLACK SKY. The wild heath below flared under the jagged light, then settled back into semi-darkness as the thunder rolled and rumbled around it. But in that brief moment, the hunched figures of three old hags could be seen.

"Where shall we three meet again?" screamed the first witch. "In thunder, lightning or in rain?"

"When the hurly-burly's done!" shrieked the second. "When the battle's lost and won!"

"At the setting of the sun," howled the third.

"Where's the place?"

"Upon the heath?"

"There to meet with Macbeth!"

These three weird sisters crouched closer together, ragged garments hanging from their scrawny bodies, and began to chant, filling the air with their howling. "Fair is foul, and foul is fair. Hover through the fog and filthy air . . . !"

King Duncan was at a camp with his attendants, awaiting news of a battle which was raging some distance away. The battle was between the King's soldiers and a rebel army who were being helped by troops from Norway. Helped also by the King's own treacherous Thane of Cawdor.

A blood-streaked sergeant burst into the King's camp with news from the battlefield. One name was repeated again and again as he told his tale of death and bravery. That name was Macbeth, the Thane of Glamis and a general in the King's army. The sergeant told of Macbeth's fearlessness in the face of the enemy, his courage and daring in the bloody battle.

Duncan listened closely and, when he heard the Thane of Cawdor had been captured, ordered that the traitor should be executed and Macbeth immediately given his title as a reward.

"Go and greet Macbeth as the new Thane of Cawdor," he told Ross and Angus, two of his noblemen.

The three witches were waiting. They were silent, but the wind whipped and wailed around them as if mimicking their own evil voices.

Then there was the sound of a drum.

"Macbeth comes!" said one of the weird sisters.

Macbeth was with another general of the King's army, his friend Banquo. The two were celebrating the victory, Banquo beating on a drum, Macbeth marching beside him, laughing.

His smile faded, however, when he saw the three hunched figures appearing out of the mist. Banquo's drumming ceased and the two men came to a halt.

"Speak, if you can!" Macbeth ordered them. "What are you?"

"All hail, Macbeth, Thane of Glamis!" said the first witch.

"All hail, Macbeth, Thane of Cawdor!" said the second.

"All hail, Macbeth, who shall be King hereafter!" said the third.

Macbeth listened, but did not understand. Thane of Glamis, yes, that was his title. But Thane of Cawdor? And *King*? He was not without his dreams, and to become King one day was one of them. But King Duncan, though an old man, was alive and well, as were his two sons, Malcolm and Donalbain. So how could Macbeth become King?

Banquo, equally puzzled by these strange pronouncements, was asking the three witches to tell him about his own future. But their predictions were even more baffling.

"Lesser than Macbeth, and greater," the first witch told him.

"Not so happy, yet much happier," said the second.

"You will be the father of kings, but not King yourself," said the third.

And the three old hags began to dissolve into the mist.

"Wait!" cried Macbeth. "Tell me more!"

But they were gone.

A silence hung over that bleak heath as the wind seemed to hold its breath. The two men looked at one another, as if sharing some wild dream. Then came the sound of someone approaching.

"Who's there?" called a nervous Banquo.

It was Ross and Angus, the two messengers from the King. They greeted Macbeth and Banquo, then told how the King had heard about Macbeth's brave deeds on the battlefield and had made him Thane of Cawdor!

Macbeth stared at them.

Banquo was first to find his voice. "What, can the devil speak the truth?"

"But the Thane of Cawdor is alive," Macbeth said to the two messengers.

"He has been sentenced to death for treason," explained Angus.

Thoughts whirled inside Macbeth's head. If one of the predictions had come true, why not the other? But he pushed away wicked ideas that began to form in his mind about how he might gain the throne. If chance would make him king, then let chance crown him.

King Duncan greeted Macbeth warmly, embraced Banquo, and thanked them both for all they had done to help secure victory in the battle. Then the King told everyone that he was making his eldest son, Malcolm, the Prince of Cumberland and thus heir to the throne.

The news was greeted with much joy by everybody except Macbeth, who hid his disappointment behind a false but fixed smile as he congratulated the young prince. Inwardly, Macbeth seethed. Were his newly fanned flames of hope to be snuffed out after all? Were his new dreams of being King to be denied so swiftly?

Duncan declared that he and his royal party would travel to Macbeth's castle that day and stay as guests for one night. Macbeth immediately expressed his delight at this news and set off ahead of the others to warn his wife and to make preparations.

Lady Macbeth was by the window of her room in the castle, clutching a letter in one hand. She already knew its contents by heart and was shaking with excitement. The letter was from her husband and told of the meeting with the three witches on the heath and how he was now Thane of Cawdor.

"And shall be King!" she promised herself. Then her excitement faltered as she remembered her husband's nature. Was he ruthless enough to do what was necessary? She was far from sure.

A messenger arrived ahead of Macbeth.

"The King comes here tonight," he told the lady of the castle.

At first shocked by this news, Lady Macbeth suddenly knew that fate had provided her with an opportunity which would have to be grasped immediately if her ambitions were to be realised. The King must never leave their castle alive.

Macbeth arrived soon after.

"My dearest love," he said. "Duncan comes here tonight."

Lady Macbeth looked directly at her husband. "And when does he go?"

"Tomorrow," replied Macbeth.

"Never let him see tomorrow," muttered his wife. She looked into Macbeth's eyes and saw that they showed his thoughts too plainly. "Put a welcome on your face," she told him. "Look like the innocent flower – but be the serpent under it!"

"We will speak about this another time," said Macbeth, evasively. His wife's ice-cold determination was making him afraid.

Lady Macbeth held his arm. "Look upright and honest," she said. "Leave all the rest to me."

When Duncan arrived, Lady Macbeth greeted him with a smile and told him what an honour it was to have the King in her house. Macbeth, too, managed to hide his fears and guilty thoughts and appear cordial. At least, for a time.

Later, snatching a few moments to himself whilst the meal was in progress, Macbeth wrestled with his feelings. "If it must be done, then it's best done quickly," he muttered to himself, pacing up and down his room. But he knew the deed he was contemplating was evil, and Macbeth had a very real fear of his crimes catching up with him at some future date. "He trusts me. I am his kinsman and one of his subjects, and he is a guest in my home. As his host, I should be protecting him not taking the knife to him myself!"

Lady Macbeth threw open the door of his room. "He has almost finished his meal!" she said urgently. "Why have you left the chamber?"

"We'll go no further in this business," Macbeth said, avoiding her eye. "He has honoured me recently, and all sorts of people now have a good opinion of me."

His wife looked at him with disgust. "Are you afraid to do what needs to be done? Are you a coward?"

"I dare do all a man dares to do?" retorted Macbeth, hotly. "But if we should fail . . . ?"

"Screw up your courage," she answered, "and we'll not fail! When Duncan is asleep, I'll see to it that his two servants are in a drunken stupor so that they do not wake. But when they do, *they* will be blamed for the deed."

Macbeth found himself being persuaded by the plan. "True! Will they not be called guilty when we have stained them with blood and used their own two daggers?"

With matters decided, he and his lady went back to the dining hall, false smiles once again concealing the evil in their hearts.

After midnight, when almost all in the castle slept, Banquo and his son, Fleance, met in the castle courtyard. Banquo's troubled thoughts were keeping him from his sleep. He saw a light.

"Who's there?" said Banquo.

"A friend." Macbeth appeared out of the darkness, a servant carrying a torch ahead of him.

"Last night, I dreamt of the three weird sisters," Banquo said to his friend. "They have shown you some truth."

"I do not think of them," Macbeth told him. "But we must speak about them at another time."

They wished each other goodnight, then Banquo and his son went back to their beds. Macbeth turned to his servant.

"Go and tell your mistress that when my drink is ready she should strike the bell," he said. "Then go to your bed."

Macbeth watched the servant leave him, then began to move towards the King's chamber.

He stopped.

A bloodstained weapon seemed to appear in front of him, turning his own blood to ice.

"Is this a dagger which I see before me, the handle towards my hand?" he mumbled, half-crazy with fear. He reached out to grasp it . . . but there was nothing to grasp, even though it still hung before his eyes.

A bell rang somewhere. It was his signal.

Now to do the evil deed.

Once again, Macbeth walked towards the King's chamber.

Lady Macbeth came into the empty courtyard. An owl shrieked, then silence settled over the night again. She glanced towards the door of the King's room, suddenly knowing what was happening inside.

"He is doing it," she said, satisfied.

Moments later, Macbeth emerged from the shadows.

"I have done the deed," he said. He looked at his hands. "This is a sorry sight."

She told him not to be foolish, but he was convinced that he would never be able to sleep again. Then she noticed that he was still holding the daggers.

"Why did you bring them from the place? They must lie there! Take them and smear the sleeping servants with blood."

But Macbeth was unnerved. "I'll go to that room no more," he said. "I'm afraid to think about what I have done, and I'll not look on it again."

She snatched the weapons from his hands. "Give me the daggers!" she hissed, and moved quickly towards Duncan's apartments.

Macbeth, in a nightmare of his own making, waited for her to come back. And as he waited he heard a knocking at the castle gate but was unable to move and could only stare at his bloody hands.

Lady Macbeth reappeared. She heard the knocking.

"I hear someone at the south gate," she whispered. "We must go to our chamber." She looked at her own hands, now the same colour as her husband's. "A little water will wash away all traces of this deed. Quick! Come! Put on your night-gown!"

And, as the urgent sound of more knocking echoed through the courtyard, the two of them hurried to their rooms.

The porter swung open the south gate to reveal two noblemen standing there. One was Macduff, the Thane of Fife. He was the first to speak.

"Is your master awake?" he asked the porter.

Then he looked up to see Macbeth coming towards the gate, a cloak thrown over his night-gown. Macbeth greeted both men.

"Is the King stirring?" asked Macduff.

"I'll bring him to you," replied Macbeth, and led them to the door of the King's chamber. He hesitated. "This is the door."

"I'll call him," said Macduff, and went into the room.

Moments later, there came a desperate shout and Macduff rushed out again.

"Horror! Horror!" he cried. "Ring the alarm bell! Murder and treason! Banquo and Donalbain! Malcolm! Awake!"

The alarm bell was rung. Chaos and confusion followed as servants and soldiers rushed everywhere. The news spread through the castle like a heath fire. The King was dead! Murdered in his bed!

The King's sons, Malcolm and Donalbain, were told of the tragedy by Macduff.

"Your royal father has been murdered," said the Thane of Fife.

"By whom?" cried Malcolm.

It was explained that the King's two servants has been found with blood on their daggers, and on their hands and faces. This was followed by an admission from Macbeth – he had since killed them both!

"Why did you do that?" demanded Macduff.

And Macduff was only the first person to suspect that Macbeth's motive for killing the servants was not simply impulsive anger and revenge, as Macbeth said it was. Later, others would have their own suspicions about him.

In no time at all the King's two sons, Malcolm and Donalbain, decided to flee the castle fearing that they too might be murdered.

Macbeth was made King. But it brought him no pleasure. He remembered the prediction of the three witches: that Banquo's children would be kings. He was also sure that Banquo suspected him of Duncan's murder. This unsettled Macbeth and he decided that something must be done.

A royal banquet was arranged at the palace. On the afternoon of the banquet, Macbeth and his wife met with Banquo.

"Are you going riding this afternoon?" Macbeth asked him.

"Aye, my good lord," replied Banquo, adding that he would be back that evening.

"Do not be late for our feast," said Macbeth.

"My lord, I will not," said Banquo.

"Is Fleance going with you?" asked Macbeth.

"Aye, my good lord," Banquo said again.

It was an opportunity Macbeth did not intend to miss. He found three desperate men whom he was able to persuade to murder Banquo and Fleance, telling them that Banquo was their enemy as well as his own, and that Banquo stood between them and their good fortune. The men were easily persuaded and quite willing to do the deed.

The attack took place on a road leading to the palace. The three murderers pounced without warning and Banquo was taken completely by surprise.

"Oh, treachery!" he cried as he was struck down. "Fly, good Fleance, fly, fly! Then avenge my death!"

Banquo's son escaped in the darkness.

At the palace, the feast was beginning. Wine flowed, and there was much merry laughter. Macbeth moved among his guests, greeting each one with a smile and a friendly word. Then he looked up and saw a face in the doorway. It was one of the murderers.

At the first opportunity, Macbeth went across to speak to the man.

"There's blood on your face!" whispered Macbeth.

"Then it's Banquo's," replied the murderer.

"Is he dead?" asked Macbeth.

"My lord, his throat is cut and there are twenty gashes to his head," came the answer.

"And Fleance?"

"He escaped," admitted the murderer.

Macbeth groaned, but he thanked the murderer for taking care of Banquo, who would never trouble him again. He went back to the table where he was immediately invited to sit down.

"The table is full," said Macbeth, looking round at the seats.

"Here is a place, sir."

"Where?"

"Here, my good lord."

Macbeth stared . . . *and saw Banquo with a gaping wound in his throat and blood all over his face*.

"Wh-which of you have done this?" Macbeth gasped.

"What, my good lord?"

Macbeth backed away from the bloody phantom, his face grey, his body shaking. "You cannot say I did it!" he wailed at the ghost.

People began to rise from their seats in readiness to leave. They were disturbed at what they saw and assumed the King had been taken ill.

"Sit, worthy friends," said Lady Macbeth, alarmed by her husband's behaviour. "My lord is often like this, and has been since childhood. The fit will last but a moment."

She hurried to Macbeth's side and began to whisper to him. "What are you doing? It's only an empty chair." For she, like the other guests, could see no ghost.

Macbeth's eyes were fixed on the chair and, briefly, the ghost went away. The King became calm for a moment, asking his guests to sit down again and to take no notice of his strange illness, which was not so strange to those who knew him. But then Banquo's ghost returned and Macbeth became so distracted and hysterical that Lady Macbeth was forced to ask everyone to leave.

After they had gone, she stared silently at her husband.

"Blood will have blood," Macbeth was muttering, certain now that he would be punished for his crimes. He looked up at his wife. "Why did Macduff not come to the feast?" He was already planning another murder, so stained by the blood of others that it no longer seemed to matter.

The three witches were in a cave. A boiling cauldron stood in the centre and the three hunched hags circled round it, chanting.

"Double, double, toil and trouble; fire burn and cauldron bubble."

As they chanted each in turn threw some ghastly, grisly ingredient into the stinking brew – eye of newt, toe of frog, tooth of wolf, tongue of dog – then danced around the sooty pot until the foul smell drenched their whole bodies.

They stopped.

One shrieked a warning. "By the pricking of my thumbs, something evil this way comes!"

Macbeth came. He had questions, but the answers were waiting for him before he could ask them. Answers which came from three shapes that appeared out of the steaming cauldron.

The first was a head wearing a helmet. "Macbeth, Macbeth, Macbeth," it said. "Beware Macduff! Beware the Thane of Fife!"

The head vanished and was replaced by a child, covered with blood. "Macbeth, Macbeth, Macbeth," it said. "Be bloody and bold. No one born of a woman shall harm Macbeth!"

This child vanished, only to be replaced by another, but this one was wearing a crown and holding a tree in its hand. "Macbeth shall never be defeated until the great Birnam Wood shall come to Dunsinane!"

"That will never be!" cried Macbeth, as the third vision faded into nothingness. For how could a *forest* march against him? There remained just one question for which Macbeth wanted an answer. "Will Banquo's descendants ever reign in this kingdom?"

"Ask no more!" chanted the three witches.

But Macbeth pressed them to answer and out of the vanishing cauldron came a procession of eight kings, all like Banquo. The last carried a mirror in his hand and in this even more kings were reflected, stretching away into the distance. The ghost of Banquo followed the procession, looking triumphant.

Macbeth had his answer.

The procession, Banquo and the three weird sisters all vanished and Macbeth was left alone in the stinking cave.

Macduff had fled to England to join Malcolm, Duncan's son. Macbeth sent murderers to Macduff's castle but found only the Thane of Fife's wife and children.

"Where is your husband?" one of the murderers asked Lady Macduff.

"I hope in a place where you cannot find him," she replied.

"He's a traitor," said the murderer.

"You lie, you villain!" cried Macduff's son.

The murderer stabbed him to death, then turned and did the same to the boy's mother. After this, the murderers killed every other person in the house.

News of the massacre reached Macduff in England. He listened with growing horror.

"All my pretty ones? Did you say all?" He was beside himself with grief.

Malcolm was with him and quickly persuaded Macduff to take his revenge on the murderous Macbeth. They would assemble an army and mount an attack on the castle at Dunsinane where Macbeth was now living.

Lady Macbeth had lost her mind.

All the horrors had swallowed up her sanity and now she walked the castle, dry-washing her hands to try and obliterate the imaginary blood which she saw on them and which would not seem to go away.

"Out damned spot!" she said, scrubbing at her hands. "Yet who would have thought the old man had so much blood in him?"

Later, she killed herself.

There was little time for Macbeth to consider his wife's death. Macduff and his army were already drawing closer to the castle. Macbeth's only comfort were the words of the ghostly infant who had told him that he could never be defeated until Birnam Wood came to Dunsinane. And how could that possibly happen?

Then a message was brought to Macbeth.

Birnam Wood was moving towards Dunsinane!

"Liar!" Macbeth screamed at the man.

But the messenger told the truth.

Macduff and his army were closing in on the castle, and each man carried before him *the branch of a tree as cover*. So Birnam Wood did indeed seem to be on the move!

Macbeth fought to the bitter end, but at last he was faced with Macduff.

"I have no words," Macduff told him. "My voice is in my sword."

"You cannot kill me!" cried Macbeth, remembering the words of the first ghost child. "I lead a charmed life which no one born of a woman can take from me!"

"Despair of your charm," Macduff told him, "for I was prematurely *taken* from my mother's womb, and so not born *of* her."

And so it was that Macbeth discovered how the three evil witches had cheated him with their warped and deceptive trickery. Nothing was left for him now, only death. With one last effort, he lifted his sword to face his assailant.

"Lay on, Macduff!" he cried. "And damned to him that first cries 'Mercy!'" Their swords crashed together.

They fought a fierce but short fight. Macduff killed Macbeth then cut off his head and carried it to Malcolm, his new King.

"Hail, King of Scotland!" cried Macduff.

"Hail, King of Scotland!" echoed the others around him.

And Malcolm acknowledged this with a sweeping bow.